# A Salute to Historic Black Abolitionists

Copyright © 1988, 1996 by Empak Publishing Company

ISBN 0-922162-5-0 (Volume V)
ISBN 0-922162-15-8 (Volume Set)

# A Salute to Historic Black Abolitionists

## EMPAK PUBLISHING COMPANY

Published by Empak Publishing Company
212 East Ohio Street, Suite 300, Chicago, IL 60611.

Publisher & Editor: Richard L. Green
Assoc. Editor: Phyllis W. Ragsdale
Researcher: Phyllis W. Ragsdale
Production: Dickinson & Associates, Inc.
Illustration: S. Gaston Dobson
Foreword: Frank B. Willis

On behalf of Empak Publishing Company, I am pleased to endorse the fifth in a special series of Black History publications, *A Salute to Historic Black Abolitionists*, produced by Empak, which gives recognition to 22 historic Black Americans who risked their lives and fortunes to lobby and toil on behalf of the cessation of slavery and the freedom of all Black Americans.

Slavery, which can be defined as involuntary servitude, the legalized social institution in which humans are held in bondage as property or chattels, existed in the United States as early as 1619, and is often referred to as America's most notorious and obnoxious sin. An inhumane occurrence that denied and suppressed the individual rights of Blacks and—in a divide and conquer quest—perpetrated the separation of family members. Slavery eventually gave rise to the abolitionist movement, which pitted states against states, and North against South.

During the course of the brutalizing slavery that existed in the United States, many laws were passed and practiced to perpetuate the institution. For example, it was illegal for slaves to learn to read or write; beat drums; conduct religious services without the presence of a White person; possess firearms; strike or. rebel against a White; own property; assemble in groups of more than five; buy or sell goods; testify in court; vote; or marry. All of these laws were employed with the ultimate goal of maintaining the economic advantage of the slave system and preserving absolute control of the slaves.

The abolitionists highlighted within this publication hailed from varied backgrounds and occupations, which accounted for their different beliefs and measures employed in combating slavery. While some abolitionists urged the use of "moral suasion" to convince the government to end slavery, some openly recommended violent rebellion, and others advocated a return to Africa (colonization). However the means, their common bond was that slavery must end, no matter what the cost.

Even though President Lincoln signed the *Emancipation Proclamation* in 1863, slavery still continued to exist in several states. However, in 1865, after the Union victory, the *Thirteenth Amendment* to the Constitution was passed, proclaiming . . . "Neither slavery nor involuntary servitude shall exist within the United States." Thus, nearly 250 years of institutionalized slavery came to an end.

This publication—*A Salute to Historic Black Abolitionists*—reminds us that this period in Black history is still important today. Much of what was sought and communicated 150 years ago, remains timely as Black Americans continue to seek full equality and first-class citizenship. The struggle undertaken by the millions of Blacks, whose toil as slaves helped build this country, must be remembered, cherished, and embraced. This is the legacy left to Black America by the courageous, historic Black abolitionists.

*Frank B. Willis*

EDITOR'S NOTE: A resident of Frederick Douglass' hometown, Rochester, NY, and a product of its school system, Frank B. Willis has served as a member of the Rochester Board of Education since 1980. Having previously held the position of vice president and president on the Board, Mr. Willis is presently a member of the Board's curriculum, personnel, and community relations committees. In addition, Mr. Willis is a current member of the Monroe County, New York State and National School Boards Associations, National Alliance of Black School Educators, Caucus of Black School Board Members, Council of Great City Schools, and Council of Urban Boards of Education.

# CONTENTS

*Editor's Note: Due to this booklet's space limitations, some facets on the lives of the above noted Historic Black Abolitionists have been omitted.*

# BISHOP RICHARD ALLEN
## (1760-1831)

*Richard Allen was one of the greatest Black religious leaders in American history. His leadership and organizational skills were phenomenal. The African Methodist Episcopal (A.M.E.) Church, which he founded, is today the oldest and largest formal institution in Black America.*

Born of slave parents in 1760, in Philadelphia, Allen taught himself to read and write after he was sold to another master in Dover, Delaware. With the permission of his master, he joined the Methodist Society and was soon heading the Society's meetings. His master's offer to allow him to purchase his own freedom spurred Allen to work as a day laborer, brick maker, and teamster. He worked until he had earned the 2,000 Continental dollars it took to make good the offer. Allen served as a wagon driver during the Revolutionary War and, in 1786, after serving as an itinerate preacher, he returned to Philadelphia to begin his ministry.

When Allen and Rev. Absalom Jones went to Philadelphia's St. George Methodist Episcopal Church on a Sunday in November 1786, a new chapter in Black history unfolded. Allen organized Black prayer meetings and encouraged greater Black attendance at St. George. As he told it: "when the colored people began to get numerous in attending the church, they moved us from the seats we usually sat on ... and told us to go in the gallery. [The] meeting had begun and ... just as we got to the seats, the elder said, 'Let us pray.' We had not been long upon our knees before I heard considerable scuffling and low talking. I raised my head up and saw one of the trustees ... having hold of the Rev. Absalom Jones, pulling him up off his knees, and saying, 'You must get up—-you must not kneel here.' Mr. Jones replied, 'Wait until the prayer is over.' " The trustee would not wait.

Before the service ended, every Black man, woman and child, led by Allen, walked out of the church. It was the first mass demonstration staged by Blacks in America! As news of the demonstration spread, Blacks in Boston, New York, and other northern cities walked out of segregated White institutions and created their own. Five months later, in April 1787, Allen and Jones responded by creating the Free African Society. The Society's varied features were those of a mutual aid society, a church, a political structure, and an insurance company.

Five years later, the Society's membership decided to build a church. This decision was not immediately acted upon because a severe yellow fever epidemic, in 1793, interrupted the plan. As others fled the city, Allen focused the Free African Society on the dreary business of recruiting Blacks to serve as nurses and undertakers. After the epidemic had run its course, the church building plan was resumed and on July 17, 1794, the Bethel Church, which later became the first African Methodist Episcopal (AME) congregation, was established. Under Allen's organization and leadership, by 1816, the AME church boasted a national membership, with Allen ordained as bishop, the first Black bishop in America.

Allen was a staunch supporter of the Anti-Slavery Societies, president of the first Negro Convention, and a contributing correspondent to the first Black newspaper, Freedom's Journal. Writing for the Journal, he eloquently opposed the American Colonization Society on the basis that "its philosophy of removal of Blacks from the United States was based on racial prejudice rather than benevolence." Yet another of Allen's major accomplishments was the organizing of the Society of Free People of Color for Promoting Instruction and School Education of Children of African Descent.

Bishop Richard Allen died on March 26, 1831. Throughout his life, Allen continued to press vigorously for the abolition of slavery. He established himself as one of the giants of Black history and, indeed, of American history.

# OSBORNE P. ANDERSON
## (1830-1871)

*A famed abolitionist, Union Army non-commissioned officer, and author, Osborne Anderson was the only one of John Brown's trusted fighting lieutenants to escape the historic raid on Harper's Ferry.*

On a Sunday night in October 1859, a small band of anti-slavery militants, led by John Brown, seized the federal arsenal at Harper's Ferry, Virginia. Their mission was to secure sufficient ammunition to carry on a full-scale revolt against Virginia slaveholders. However, within a matter of hours, an informer had alerted the entire countryside. Both federal and state troops were dispatched. The next day, Brown and his men were overtaken. Among the rebels were at least five Blacks. Four were killed at Harper's Ferry or later hanged. One, Osborne Perry Anderson, escaped.

Osborne Anderson was born free in 1830, in Chester County, Pennsylvania. He received a public school education and later attended Oberlin College in Ohio. In 1850, Anderson moved to Canada, where he learned the trade of printing, a skill which later proved useful in his subsequent abolitionist activities.

In the spring of 1858 in Chatham, Ontario, Anderson met the revolutionary White abolitionist, John Brown. Brown organized a convention in Chatham as a preliminary step toward overthrowing slavery in the United States. At the time, there were some 30,000 Blacks, fugitive slaves and free people living in Canada. Many attended the convention, including Osborne Anderson. Because of his excellent writing skills, Anderson served as the recording secretary at some of the convention's secret meetings. Later, he was elected a member of Brown's provisional congress.

The raid at Harper's Ferry was intended to be the first step in a plan to establish an independent state of freed slaves in the Appalachian region of the United States. As the sole survivor of the raid, Anderson provided an invaluable, written account of the planning and execution of the event. His 1861 book, *A Voice From Harper's Ferry*, describes the conditions on the farm which John Brown rented to prepare his men for the raid. Just five miles from Harper's Ferry, military supplies and equipment were stashed, and a small band of rebels was secretly assembled and trained.

On October 16, 1859, the day of the raid, Anderson and Albert Hazlett were ordered to guard a key position at the arsenal. When it became clear to Anderson and Hazlett that the raid would not succeed, both managed to escape. However, Hazlett was later captured and put to death. Anderson managed to elude his pursuers by escaping to a river and from there, he made his way to Philadelphia. Once there, friends helped him out of the country, back to Canada.

The raid at Harper's Ferry sent shock waves through the slaveholding South and fueled anti-slavery agitation in the North and in Canada. *A Voice From Harper's Ferry* helped all to understand the full meaning of the raid and the bravery of the men who enacted it. In particular, it exposed the cowardice of the slaveholders and militia who guarded the arsenal. Anderson wrote: "They had not pluck enough to fight, nor to use the well-loaded arms in their possession, but were concerned rather in keeping a whole skin by parleying (sic), or in spilling cowardly tears, to excite pity ... and in that way escape merited punishment."

A year after the Harper's Ferry incident, Anderson paid his respects to John Brown by visiting his grave site in New York. As a non-commissioned officer in the Union Army during the Civil Way, he continued to fight for an end to slavery. Osborne Anderson died in Washington, D.C. in 1871, at the age of forty-one.

# HENRY W. BIBB
## (1815-1854)

*Henry Bibb, a fugitive slave, later became a noted newspaper editor, abolitionist lecturer, and an influential author.*

"To be compelled to stand by and see you whip and slash my wife without mercy, when I could afford her no protection ... My infant child was also frequently flogged by Mrs. Gatewood for crying, until its skin was bruised literally purple. This kind of treatment was what drove me from home and family, to seek a better home for them." These were the bitter words of Henry W. Bibb in a letter to his former master, W.H. Gatewood. Like so many fugitive slaves, he had hoped to be able to gain freedom for his family. But Henry never saw his wife and children again.

Henry Bibb was born into slavery of mixed parentage in 1815. His mother, Mildred Jackson, was a slave; his father was State Senator James Bibb. Henry so abhorred slavery that he tried to escape six times and was considered such an incorrigible slave that he had six different owners. Whenever he successfully escaped, he returned to try and help his family flee. Unfortunately, he was never able to gain his family's freedom. Finally, in desperation, he made up his mind that he must be free at any cost, even at the loss of his family. In 1842, he escaped to Detroit. Michigan's anti-slavery leaders attempted to aid him in his efforts to free his wife, but they were unsuccessful.

From 1842 to 1844, Bibb toured Michigan and the Northeastern part of the United States, lecturing against slavery and campaigning for the Liberty party. The party had been established, in 1840, by anti-slavery leaders, one of whom, James G. Birney, ran unsuccessfully for the U.S. presidency in 1840 and 1844. The noted White abolitionist, William Lloyd Garrison, became familiar with Bibb's unique speaking skills and ranked him with Frederick Douglass as one of the best qualified to speak on the subject of slavery. It is reported that, following one of Bibb's speeches, the audience cheered, clapped, stamped, laughed, and wept by turns.

In 1848, having given up the hope of ever joining his family, Bibb married Mary Miles of Boston. During this period, he also worked diligently to produce his book, *The Narrative of the Life and Adventures of Henry Bibb: An American Slave*. Bibb's *Narrative* was published in 1849. Among other topics, it detailed the sexual exploitation of Black women by their slave masters because, during Bibb's enslavement, a slave trader had forced his wife to become a prostitute.

After the passage of the *Fugitive Slave Act*, Bibb and his new wife fled to Canada where, in 1851, he established Canada's first Black newspaper, *Voice of the Fugitive*. It was here that Josiah Henson and a group of White philanthropists became the sponsors of a Refugee Home Society plan. The basis of the plan was that the Society was to purchase 50,000 acres to be divided into twenty-five acre plots for sale to individual families. One third of all revenues was to be used for educational purposes, and no settler could sell his land in less than fifteen years; if abandoned, it reverted back to the Society.

Bibb also founded and served as president of the North American Convention of Colored People, which denounced the American Colonization Society, as well as the *Fugitive Slave Act*. The convention established the American Continental and West India League, which were Pan-African efforts designed to unite free Black people.

Henry W. Bibb died in 1854, at the age of 39. However, during his short life he made lasting contributions to the abolitionist movement in Canada and the United States. Henry W. Bibb's name remains significant in the annals of Black American history.

# WILLIAM WELLS BROWN
## (c. 1814-1884)

*William Wells Brown was a physician, author, historian and literary giant. His most notable historical books were The Black Man, His Antecedents, His Genius And His Achievements (1863), and The Rising Son; Or, the Antecedents and Advancement of the Colored Race (1874).*

William Wells Brown was born in Lexington, Kentucky. William's mother was a slave, and his father was a slaveholder. It was rumored that Daniel Boone was his grandfather. In 1834, Brown escaped from slavery to Ohio, where he was provided refuge by a Quaker named Wells Brown who suggested that William use his name. Thus, he acquired the middle name of Wells and the surname of Brown.

Brown settled in Ohio, where he labored hard to educate himself. One of his jobs, as a steward aboard steamboats on Lake Erie, enabled him to help other fugitives escape to freedom. In 1834, he married Elizabeth Schooner of Cleveland. The Browns had three daughters, one of whom died in infancy. His youngest daughter, Josephine, became one of his biographers. In 1847, William and Elizabeth separated, and he took custody of their two children.

From 1843 to 1849, William Wells Brown served the abolitionist movement as a lecturing agent for the Anti-Slavery Societies in New York and Massachusetts, and he was an Underground Railroad agent. In 1849, he went to Europe as a representative to the American Peace Society in Paris. While in Europe, he tried to win British support for the abolitionist movement. From September 1849 to September 1854, he remained in Great Britain, where he traveled more than 25,000 miles and delivered more than a thousand lectures.

Like Frederick Douglass, Brown's English associates helped him to legally secure his freedom. He later returned to America, in 1854, to continue his fight against slavery. Brown recruited Black soldiers in Massachusetts, New York, Pennsylvania, and New Jersey to join the Union Army. After the Civil War, he became an apprentice-trained physician. However, Brown devoted more time to writing and publishing, and his reputation thereafter became linked to literature.

Brown wrote more than a dozen books and pamphlets. His first book, in 1847, was an autobiography; *Narrative of William W. Brown, A Fugitive Slave, Written by Himself*. Brown also authored three major works which were held in the highest esteem in the United States and Europe. One of his earlier historical biographies, which appeared in 1855, was titled *St. Domingo: Its Revolution and its Patriots*. The book highlighted the rise and fall of the Haitian freedom fighter, Toussaint L'Ouverture.

The Black Man contained fifty-three biographical sketches of prominent Black men, including Nat Turner, William Still, William C. Nell, Frederick Douglass and other Black men of stature. The book also refuted the inferiority of the Black man and praised the anti-slavery movement. *The Rising Son* provided a general history of the Black American from his African beginnings. The book also addressed the beatings, sufferings, murders, rapes, and other deplorable acts attributed to the institution of slavery.

William Wells Brown also wrote *Clotel; Or, The President's Daughter: A Narrative of Slavery in the United States*, published in 1853. It was the first novel produced by a Black American, and its tale, loosely based on the relationship between Thomas Jefferson and his slave concubine Sally Hemings, was so controversial that the 1853 version, published in London, was not published in the United States until 1969. Brown was also the first Black to publish a drama, *The Escape; Or, A Leap for Freedom*, in 1858.

William Wells Brown, a literary giant and human rights activist, died on November 6, 1884, in Chelsea, a suburb of Boston. He was survived by his second wife and his two daughters.

# REV. ALEXANDER CRUMMEL
## (1819-1898)

*Freeborn, Alexander Crummel was an Episcopal priest, missionary to West Africa, professor, and co-founder of the American Negro Academy. Crummel was exceptional among the many notable Black abolitionists. Although he never actually shared the direct experience of slavery as did some of his contemporary abolitionists, he shared their fervor for Black emancipation.*

Alexander Crummel was exceptional among the many notable Black abolitionists. Although he was of pure African descent, he hailed from a long line of freeborn Blacks in New York City. He never came close to the direct experience of slavery as had some of his more notable contemporaries—men like Frederick Douglass, Henry Highland Garnet, and Martin Delany. Yet, he shared their fervor for Black emancipation. And, although he marched to the beat of a somewhat different drummer, he fully embraced the abolitionist spirit and activity of the era.

Extremely brilliant, Crummel may well have been the most well-educated Black man in America during the 1800s. Born in 1819, as a child he attended the African Free School of New York, the Canal Street High School, and Noyes Academy in New Hampshire. He studied for four years, at Oneida Theological Institute where, with the fiery Henry Garnet as a classmate, he graduated in 1839. That same year, Crummel applied for admission to General Theological Seminary in New York. He was rejected because of his race.

Crummel decided early in life that he would become a minister. True to himself, in spite of the rejection, for the next four years, he studied privately under the tutelage of several of America's leading Episcopal clergymen. By 1844, he was an ordained Episcopal priest. From 1848 to 1853, Crummel lived in England, where he lectured, raised money for the construction of a church in New York, and continued his studies at Queen's College.

Throughout his years of formal study, Crummel managed

to remain active in anti-slavery efforts. As a boy of 10 he had eloquently addressed the New Hampshire Anti-Slavery Society. Before reaching age 20, he had served as secretary to the society's New York State chapter. In 1840, Crummel attended an anti-slavery convention in Albany, New York, and later drafted a petition to New York's state legislature to remove voting restrictions on Blacks. He promoted the establishment of Black colleges and worked with Frederick Douglass to frame an agenda for abolishing slavery. Crummel's scholarly pursuits and his commitment made him a valuable ally in the cause of freedom.

When Crummel left England in 1853, he went to Liberia as a missionary of the Episcopal church. He spent nearly 20 years in Africa preaching, teaching, and organizing churches. Crummel had become convinced that Africa was a far better place for Blacks than the oppressive United States. During the Civil War years, consistent with this conviction, he made several trips to the United States to encourage Black emigration and to generate financial support for education in Liberia. It is in this regard that Crummel differed with his Black abolitionist friends. Most of them opposed emigration and the efforts of the American Colonization Society to foster it. Crummel, on the other hand, worked with the Society.

Crummel returned to America for good in 1872. Due to ideological conflict with his colleagues in Liberia, he had been dismissed from his academic post at the new Liberia College in Monrovia. His decision to leave was further prompted by mounting political strife in Liberia and his inability to establish his own school there. Shortly after his return to the United States, Crummel founded St. Luke's Episcopal Church in Washington, D.C. He also taught for two years at Howard University.

In 1897, Crummel co-founded, with some 40 other Black leaders, the American Negro Academy. The Academy was the first Black scholarly and artistic organization in the country. Its membership included the great thinker, W.E.B. Du Bois, and one of America's greatest poets, Paul Laurence Dunbar. As he approached the final year of his life, Crummel could look back with pride on his many accomplishments. A true scholar and visionary, Alexander Crummel continued his work until the time of his death, September 10, 1898, at the age of 79.

# MARTIN R. DELANY
## (1812-1885)

*Martin Robinson Delany's inquiring mind, indomitable spirit, and intellectual ability combined to make him one of the most influential and controversial leaders of the abolitionist era. During the course of his lifetime, he was an author, physician, abolitionist, colonizationist, and army officer. His militant, Black nationalist views on the treatment of Black Americans established a unique place for him in history.*

Delany was born on May 6, 1812, in Charles Town, West Virginia. His father, Samuel, was a slave; his mother, Pati (Peace) Delany, was freeborn. As a small child, Martin heard his grandmother, Graci Peace, tell many proud tales of his African heritage and his royal forebears, which were among the great Golah and Mandingo tribes of Africa. In an era when Black people were bitterly scorned, Martin Delany learned to be proud of his Blackness and his heritage.

In 1822, Pati Delany took her five children and fled to West Virginia to avoid imprisonment because a Yankee book peddler had been teaching them to read. She took her children north, across the Mason-Dixon line, to the free soil of Chambersburg, Pennsylvania. A year later, Samuel Delany bought his freedom and rejoined his family. Meanwhile, young Martin and the other Delany children were able to continue their education.

At the age of 19, Delany left home and traveled on foot across the Allegheny Mountains to Pittsburgh, where he remained until 1856. While there, he studied at an African Methodist Episcopal night school. He also studied medicine and, under the tutelage of a White physician, became qualified to practice a variety of medical procedures which were common at that time. In addition, Delany later became an officer of the Pittsburgh Anti-Slavery Society, an Underground Railroad activist, and the organizer of various literary and "moral reform" groups among the growing number of fugitive slaves settling in Pittsburgh. In 1836, he served as delegate to a "colored convention," traveling both to Philadelphia and to New York in this capacity.

During this period, Delany married Catherine Richards. The couple had seven children, six boys and a girl, each named in honor of great Blacks in history. For instance, two of the boys were named Toussaint L'Ouverture and Alexander Dumas, and the girl was named Ethiopia Halle. Shortly after his marriage in 1843, Delany began publishing the first Black newspaper, west of the Alleghenies. Five years later, this excellent paper, *The Mystery,* went out of business for lack of financial support.

Delany then joined Frederick Douglass as co-editor of the *North Star.* In addition to writing for Douglass' paper, Delany was extremely active in speaking to anti-slavery gatherings throughout the East and Midwest. He made as many as three speeches a day, then, at great danger to himself, traveled on horseback at night in order to get to the next town. On one occasion, in Ohio, he barely escaped being lynched for his Black nationalist, anti-slavery remarks.

After more than a year as co-editor of the *North Star,* Delany resigned to continue his medical studies in Pittsburgh. Rejected by the Pennsylvania and New York medical schools, in 1850, he was admitted to Harvard. Hardly a month had passed before White students petitioned against his attendance. Delany was expelled, but undaunted, he continued to study medicine under the direction of two sympathetic White physicians. In 1851, he returned to Pittsburgh and used his medical knowledge to combat a tragic cholera epidemic in that city.

In 1852, Delany published the first Black nationalist treatise, *The Condition, Elevation, Emigration* and *Destiny of the Colored People of the United States, Politically Considered.* It drew harsh and immediate criticism from White abolitionists, the liberal press, and even Black leaders. Frederick Douglass, for example, conveniently ignored it. Probably as a result of Delany's work, Douglass once commented: "I thank God for making me a man, but Delany thanks him for making him a Black man." *Condition, Elevation, Emigration* urged Black separation from Whites and recommended Black resettlement in Central America, Africa, or South America. It criticized the abolitionists' lack of commitment to Black equality and justice. The book also spoke of the proud history of the Black race at a time when leading theorists debated Blacks' innate inferiority.

Delany's activities, after 1852, were typically energetic and wide-ranging. In August 1854, he attracted more than 100 men and women to a National Emigration Convention in Cleveland. By 1858, at the convention's third meeting, Delany proposed and received approval for a three-year study, the "Topographical, Geological, and Geographical Examination of the Valley of the River Niger." In the meantime, Delany moved his family to Ontario, Canada, where thousands of fugitive slaves were settling to escape the grasp of the slave-catchers encouraged by the *Fugitive Slave Act.* In 1859, Delany left Canada to journey to Africa and begin his emigration study.

Delany traveled to Abbeokuta (a city-state in present-day Nigeria), where he was able to finalize a treaty with the tribal king, allowing Black Americans to establish a self-controlled colony in the region. He later visited businessmen and noblemen in England and Scotland, where he was invited to speak to the prestigious Royal Geographical Society and the International Statistical Congress. In the face of an American delegate's abusive remarks about his presence, Delany boldly stated to Prince Albert and the rest of the assembly, "I assure your Royal Highness and his Lordship that I am a man."

Upon his return to North America in 1861, Delany made a defiant but unsuccessful effort to recruit Black emigrants for the proposed colony. However, the Emigration Convention did not specifically approve of emigration, particularly to West Africa. Delany also found time to publish chapters of a new novel, *Blake, The Huts of Africa,* in serial form in the *Anglo-African* magazine, and he wrote his *Official Report of the Niger Valley Exploring Party.*

Between 1861 and 1885, Delany practiced medicine, wrote books and articles, and worked for the betterment of Black Americans. He was commissioned as a major in the Union Army, the first Black man to hold such a rank. He also served in the Freedman's Bureau, a governmental commission established to help newly freed slaves. He later fought political corruption as a trial justice.

Delany also wrote several essays about the Civil War, American policies toward Africa, and the destiny of the Black man in America. He also worked for the Exodus Company to promote Black resettlement in Liberia and, in 1879, he completed *Principia of Ethnology: The Origin of Races and Color.*

*Principia's* analysis of the presence of Black people in the Bible, Egyptian sculpture, and other African achievements demonstrated, according to Delany, that "the builders of the pyramids, sculptors of the sphinxes and original god-kings were blacks."

Martin Delany died in Xenia, Ohio on January 24, 1885. Within the span of his 73 years, he accomplished the work of several lifetimes. This proud, industrious man, who believed so deeply in the greatness of Black people, was a forerunner to such Black leaders as Marcus Garvey, Dr. Martin Luther King, Jr., and Malcolm X. Martin Delany is a shining example of the character and spirit of great men.

# ■■■ FREDERICK AUGUSTUS DOUGLASS ■■■
## (c. 1817-1895)

*Slave born, Frederick Douglass became a fugitive, commanding anti-slavery lecturer, journalist, author, US Marshall, Recorder of Deeds, Minister to Haiti, and one of the most renowned, persuasive Black abolitionists in this country and abroad.*

Agitate! Agitate! Agitate! These were the famous bywords of Frederick Augustus Douglass, the means by which he believed Black Americans must unconditionally struggle for equal rights. In fact, Douglass once explained, "This struggle may be a moral one; it may be a physical one; or it may be both moral and physical. But it must be a struggle. Power concedes nothing without a demand."

Douglass was born into slavery in 1817, near Tuckahoe, Maryland. Because his slave mother, Harriet Bailey, used to call him her "little valentine," he adopted February 14th as his birthday, not knowing the exact date of his birth. He knew very little about his mother, since she was employed as a field hand on a plantation some 12 miles away, and she died when he was 8 or 9 years old. Douglass knew even less about his father, but it was rumored that he was the son of his White slave master, Aaron Anthony.

Young Fred was grossly mistreated. To keep from starving, on many occasions, he competed with his master's dogs for table scraps and bones. In 1825, he was sent to serve as a houseboy in the home of Hugh and Sophia Auld in Baltimore. Mrs. Auld grew fond of him and sought to teach him to read and write. By the time her irate husband discovered the deed and put a stop to it, Douglass had acquired enough of the rudiments to carry on by himself.

Douglass' life in Baltimore was interrupted in 1832, when he was passed along to another master and sent back to Tuckahoe's brutal plantation environment. Four years later, he, along with several other slaves, attempted to escape. However, their effort proved unsuccessful when one of the slaves revealed their plan. Viewed as a "bad slave," Frederick was then sent to a slave breaker who worked and whipped him mercilessly. He endured the mistreatment until one day he could stand it no longer and fought back.

Soon thereafter, Douglass was again sent to Baltimore, where he met Anna Murray. His love for and encouragement from Anna, a free Black woman, heightened his quest to be a free man. On September 3, 1838, Douglass, dressed in a sailor's uniform and carrying identification papers provided by a free Black seaman, managed to reach New York City. There, he met David Ruggles, an abolitionist, who sheltered Douglass and assisted him with his wedding plans. Frederick changed his surname from Bailey to Douglass, married Anna Murray, and the couple moved to New Bedford, Massachusetts.

Douglass began reading the *Liberator* and frequenting anti-slavery meetings, and on one occasion was unexpectedly called upon to speak. In the presence of some of the most prominent abolitionists, William Lloyd Garrison, Wendell Phillips, and William Collins, Douglass told his story, and he was immediately urged to become an anti-slavery lecturer.

Douglass' towering, erect posture depicted dignity and strength, and when he spoke, his voice was a rich, powerful baritone. These attributes, when taken together, gave Douglass quite a commanding presence. Yet, he provided more than a mere presence. His enunciation and command of the English language armed him with a profound argument, which he reinforced by employing a quick wit and vivid imagery to describe the horror of slavery.

So eloquent were Douglass' speeches that after a while the public began to wonder if this well-versed man was ever a slave. At the risk of capture, Douglass chose to remove this doubt by publishing an account of his slave experiences, *Narrative of the Life of Frederick Douglass*, in 1845. His freedom jeopardized by the detailed documentation presented in his book, Douglass fled to England and remained overseas for two years.

With the financial aid of his European friends, Douglass returned to America, legally secured his freedom, and launched his newspaper, the *North Star*. Douglass wrote scathing editorials on a variety of topics; slavery was just one of his targets.

About the need to remain adamantly concerned about the plight of slaves, he wrote: "Those who profess to favor freedom, and yet deprecate agitation, are men who want crops without plowing up the ground."

In an effort to attack job discrimination against Blacks, Douglass wrote, "we need mechanics as well as ministers; we must build as well as live in houses; we must construct bridges as well as pass over them." He responded to the *Fugitive Slave Act* of 1850, by writing that the "true remedy" to the legislation was a "good revolver, a steady hand, and a determination to shoot down any man attempting to kidnap a fugitive slave." During this period, Douglass also found time to publish his second autobiography, *My Bondage and My Freedom*, in 1855.

Douglass was a man of action, as well. His previous belief in "moral suasion" was becoming unsatisfactory to him, and he began implementing more active ways to show his convictions. He focused attention on Jim Crow laws in the North, by entering public places in which he knew these laws were enforced, sometimes risking physical ejection. He also gave his money to aid fugitive slaves, and used his printing shop in Rochester, New York as an Underground Railroad station.

In addition, he became impressed with the radical abolitionist, John Brown, whose advocacy of revolutionary means to end slavery, intrigued Douglass. However, he decided against joining Brown in his plan to overthrow the government. Still, his involvement with Brown was visible enough that a warrant for Douglass' arrest was issued after the Harper's Ferry raid, and Douglass had to again flee; this time, he went to Canada for several months.

However, he returned with a vengeance. Douglass saw political organizing as an important way for his people to shape their own destiny, so he attended several conventions of abolitionists, Blacks, and reformers. He welcomed the outbreak of the Civil War because he saw "little hope for the freedom of slaves" without it. Subsequently, as a recruiting agent for the Union Army, he signed up two of his sons, Charles and Lewis.

The end of slavery did not still Douglass. His voice and pen addressed various issues, including world peace, women's rights, and full civil rights for Blacks. His political efforts were rewarded when, from 1871 to 1891, Douglass served in four significant government posts. During this period, he received criticism for being on the federal payroll. One critic charged that "a fat office gagged him."

However, Douglass' barbed attacks persisted, because as he said in 1883: "Though we have had ... abolition ... in all the relations of life and death we are met by the color line. We cannot ignore it if we would, and ought not if we could. It hunts us at midnight, it denies us ... justice in the courts; excludes our children from schools; refuses our sons the chance to learn trades, and compels us to pursue such labor as will bring us the least reward."

Douglass died on February 20, 1895, of a heart attack. Active until the end, he had given a speech to the National Council of Women on the day of his death. The respect that Douglass commanded earned him several posthumous honors. The federal government performed three such tributes: in 1955, Douglass' home in Anacostia, D.C. was purchased as a national shrine under the National Park Service; a bridge in Washington, D.C. was named after him, and a commemorative stamp was issued in 1967.

A few days after his death, Blacks in Americus, Georgia paid their respects to this righteous man by saying: "No people who can produce a Douglass need despair."

# CHARLOTTE L. FORTEN
## (1837-1915)

*Although born into wealth and a privileged life, Charlotte Forten dedicated her life to the abolitionist cause and the moral and intellectual improvement of her people. Charlotte Forten was the grand-daughter of Jaynes Forten, daughter of Robert Forten, and niece of Robert Purvis, all of whom were wealthy, noted Black abolitionists.*

Charlotte was born in Philadelphia, in 1837. Her mother died when Charlotte was very young. She led a protected life. For example, she was not permitted to attend Philadelphia's segregated schools. Instead, the Forten family wealth allowed her to have private tutors. In order to expand her education, her father later sent her to live with another prominent Black abolitionist duo, Charles and Sarah Remond of Salem, Massachusetts. Charlotte graduated from Higginson Grammar School in 1855. She completed additional studies at Salem Normal School in 1856.

In Massachusetts, as in her home state of Pennsylvania, Charlotte moved in the elite intellectual, cultural, and abolitionist circles. Her admirers and role models included William Lloyd Garrision, Wendell Phillips, John Greenleaf Whittier, the Remonds, and other notable writers and abolitionists. Steeped in anti-slavery rhetoric and thought, as a result of her exposure to such leaders, Charlotte joined the local Anti-Slavery Society, in the same year she graduated from Higginson Grammar School, at the age of 18.

In 1856, Charlotte received a teaching assignment at the integrated Epes Grammar School, making her the first Black teacher of White students in the conservative and aristocratic bastions of Salem, Massachusetts. She taught at Epes for two years until illness forced her to resign. In 1858, she returned home to Philadelphia. Throughout the remainder of her life, she was in frail health due to lung fever. As she recuperated, Charlotte began writing. She served as a correspondent for the *National Anti-Slavery Standard* and the *Atlantic Monthly*. One of her poems, "Glimpses of England," was highly acclaimed.

For ten years, from 1854 to 1864, Charlotte kept a diary. Later published, in 1951, as *The Journal of Charlotte L. Forten,* it provided important insights into the many prominent figures who shaped her life. Her diary also revealed her thoughts about issues affecting Philadelphia's Blacks. In one entry, she wrote that she was "perfectly sick" of the behavior of some of Philadelphia's "colored" people. In an 1857 entry, she echoed Frederick Douglass' sentiments about Blacks celebrating the 4th of July. She wrote: "The celebration of this day! What a mockery it is! My soul sickens of it."

During the Civil War, Charlotte participated in a project at Port Royal, South Carolina, which was designed to help educate the hoards of destitute, illiterate slaves set free by the *Emancipation Proclamation.* Aside from teaching the freed Blacks, in July 1863, after the attack on Fort Wagner, South Carolina, she tended to the soldiers, mended their clothes, and wrote letters for them. This activity weakened her health. From late July to mid-October 1863, Charlotte traveled by sea to New York, Philadelphia, Boston, Salem, and Byberry, where she visited with friends during her attempt to regain her health.

At 41 years of age, Charlotte married Francis Grimke, an author, student of law, and a scholarly minister who used his church as a civil rights platform. Francis Grimke was much younger than Charlotte, but he loved her deeply. He described Charlotte as "one of the dearest, sweetest, loveliest spirits that ever graced this planet." Sadly, their only child died during its infancy.

Charlotte L. Forten Grimke died on July 23, 1915, at age 78, after suffering a stroke. She was survived by her husband, who never remarried after her death.

# REV HENRY HIGHLAND GARNET
## (1815-1882)

*Throughout the history of Blacks in America, Black churchmen have been at the forefront of efforts to protect, educate, and liberate their people. Henry Garnet was a Presbyterian minister and militant abolitionist, from Troy, New York, who exhorted his people to open rebellion against slavery.*

Garnet was born into slavery in New Market, Kent County, Maryland, on December 23, 1815. He was the grandson of a Mandingo chieftain. At age nine, his family escaped from slavery and eventually found a home in New York City. By age eleven, Garnet was enrolled at African Free School #1, in order to get both an academic and moral education. He later attended the Noyes Academy in Canaan, New Hampshire, and Oneida Theological Institute in Whitesboro, New York, where he graduated with honors in 1840.

During this period, Garnet became interested in the activities of the First Colored Presbyterian Church, where he met Rev. Theodore S. Wright, the·church's pastor and one of New York's leading Abolitionists. Wright welcomed Garnet into the church and baptized him. He also performed the ceremonies when Garnet married Julia Williams in 1842. With Wright's encouragement, Garnet decided to join the ministry.

The National Negro Convention was held from August 21 to 24, 1843. Among the many delegates were such notable figures as Frederick Douglass, William Wells Brown, Charles L. Remond, and other prominent abolitionists. It was here that young Henry Highland Garnet delivered a call to rebellion that unsettled the conservative Black leadership of the era, drew national attention, and established Garnet as one of the most militant abolitionists.

Garnet was an ardent supporter of the dynamic and extremely militant David Walker. In an eloquent appeal in which he, like Walker,called upon Blacks to unite in open rebellion, he said; "Brethren, arise, arise! Strike for your lives and liberties ... Let every slave throughout the land do and the days of slavery are numbered. You cannot be more op pressed than you have been, you cannot suffer greater cruelties than you have already. Rather die free men than live to be slaves." The delegates rose to their feet and the audito rium was filled with applause.

In the deliberations which followed, none other than Frederick Douglass emerged as the chief opponent to Garnet's appeal. Yet, Garnet had delivered his appeal with such skill and so convincingly that it could not easily be ignored. When it was put to a vote, the subdued majority defeated the mili tant proposition by only a single vote. Later, however, John Brown, the White radical abolitionist, was so taken by Gar net's remarks that he had them published and circulated at his own expense.

Garnet's appeal at the convention was a high point in his life. Later, from 1843 to 1848, he served as pastor of the Liberty Street Presbyterian Church in New York. Garnet traveled to Europe in 1850, where he stayed for about three years, becoming fluent in both French and German. Upon the death of his good friend Theodore Wright, he assumed the pastorate of Wright's last church, the Shiloh Presbyterian Church. Some years later, in 1865, he was the first Black to address the U.S. House of Representatives.

On November 4, 1881, Garnet's lifelong dream of traveling to Africa was fulfilled. President James A. Garfield appointed him Minister Resident and Counsel General to Liberia. How ever, shortly after arriving in Africa, he suffered an asthma attack and he never recovered. He died on February 13, 1882, at the age of 67, and was laid to rest in the land of his ances tors—Africa.

# PRINCE HALL
## (1735-1807)

*Prince Hall was a pre-revolutionary Methodist minister; revolutionary soldier with troops on Breed's Hill; fraternal leader; and chartered founder of the first Black Masonic Order.*

The early life of Prince Hall have been disputed by some historians. However, there is general agreement that Hall was born in Barbados in 1735, of mixed parentage, and that he immigrated to Boston in 1765. He enlisted in the militia during the Revolutionary War.

In spite of the disagreement about the facts of Hall's beginnings, the record of his Masonic activities is clear. Prince Hall was this country's first Black Mason. He was initiated on March 6, 1775, in Lodge No. 441, located near Boston. Shortly afterward, Hall and the 14 other Blacks who were initiated with him were given a temporary permit to meet in accordance with established Masonic practices. As Grand Master, Hall later petitioned and received approval for the establishment of African Lodge No. 459, "a regular Lodge of Free and accepted Masons, under the title or denomination of the African Lodge."

Hall immediately turned his attention to the organization of other Black lodges. By 1798, he had established three of them, which together constituted the Prince Hall Solidarity. The third lodge was established with Absalom Jones as worshipful master, and the great abolitionist minister, Richard Allen, as treasurer. In addition to his activities as a Mason, Prince Hall also worked diligently to abolish slavery and to secure equal rights for Blacks in America.

Hall was very skillful in using legal means to combat slavery and discrimination. He petitioned the Massachusetts state legislature several times. On January 13, 1777, when Hall and several other Black Masons appealed for the abolition of slavery, the state legislature refused to act. Ten years later, in February 1788, Hall appealed for legislative action to ensure that Black citizens be allowed to walk the streets in safety. Within a month the legislature passed an act "to prevent the slave trade, and for granting relief to the families of such unhappy persons as may be kidnapped or destroyed from this Commonwealth."

Prince Hall was also one of the early proponents of Black colonization. Due to what he described as the "very disagreeable and disadvantageous circumstances" of Blacks, Prince Hall and 11 members of his lodge proposed to the Massachusetts legislature that a separate state abroad be created and run by Blacks. The scheme included the raising of funds from churches or other groups to provide for travel to Africa, the purchase of land, and other activities. The goal was for the colonizers to civilize, as Hall put it; "those nations who are now sunk in ignorance and barbarity." This was perhaps the first major statement on Black colonization, a theme which would continue throughout the next two centuries in Black America.

Unable to obtain support for colonization, Hall turned his attention to the plight of Blacks in this country. He became involved in politics. As a regular taxpayer, he sued for equal educational facilities for Black children. Although this appeal was rejected, in 1798, a group of concerned Black parents opened a school in Hall's home. The site of the school was later moved to the African Meeting House, where it operated for 29 years. As the years passed, in addition to his Masonic duties and civil rights activities, Hall became an ordained minister and a successful businessman.

Partially as a result of Prince Hall's dedication, by 1977, there were 40 grand lodges, more than 5500 lodges, and half a million Black Masons in the United States, all under the name "Prince Hall." Hall died in 1807. The Black Masons, public school children, and every Black American owe a debt of gratitude to this great Black leader.

# REV. JOSIAH HENSON
## (1789-1883)

*Josiah Henson, an escaped slave, Methodist minister, Underground Railroad conductor, abolitionist orator, is believed to have been the model of history's most controversial literary works, Uncle Tom's Cabin.*

Josiah Henson was born into slavery on June 15, 1789, in Charles County, Maryland. He was rewarded by several different masters for his obedient service by being promoted to "manager" and "superintendent." On one occasion, while attempting to protect his drunken master, Henson was beaten so severely that he was never again able to raise his hands above his head. Yet, this "model" slave, who so dutifully carried out the will of his various masters, would one day run away to become an important figure in the abolitionist movement.

After being sold from master to master, Henson, his first wife, and their small children escaped to Cincinnati. Henson became a self-proclaimed minister, as a result of the training he had received from a Methodist preacher on one of the plantations. In 1828, he was admitted into the ministry of the Methodist Episcopal Church. Later, a Scottish boatman, named Burnham, helped Henson and his family travel to Buffalo, New York, and from there they were able to escape to Canada.

Taught to read and write by one of his sons (Tom), Henson published, in 1849, one of the most famous slave narratives, *The Life of Josiah Henson*. The 1879 enlarged edition, *Truth Stranger than Fiction: An Autobiography of the Rev. Josiah Henson*, carried a preface by Harriet Beecher Stowe, with introductory notes by Wendell Phillips. Both Stowe and Phillips were leading abolitionists in the White community. Josiah described in agonizing detail the effects of slavery and, in particular, the devastating consequences of separating mothers from their children in the nasty business of the slave trade. His narrative sold more than 100,000 copies, and Harriet Stowe drew from it to create her own literary bombshell, *Uncle Tom's Cabin.*

Published in 1852, *Uncle Tom's Cabin* so dramatized the evils of slavery that some historians have listed it among the causes of the Civil War. It correctly identified the slave as victim and fueled anti-slavery sentiment in the North. The usage of the term, "Uncle Tom," is still applied to non-aggressive, docile Black men. Yet, Josiah Henson was not the "Uncle Tom" some viewed him to be. He believed the institution of slavery turned "the slave into the cringing, treacherous, false, and thieving victim of tyranny."

Henson lectured throughout the northern part of the United States as well as Canada regarding the ills of slavery. He was also very active as an Underground Railroad agent, and was credited with helping 118 slaves escape to freedom. In addition, during the Canadian Rebellion of 1837-38, he served as a captain in the 2nd Essex Company of Colored Volunteers.

In 1842, Henson helped to organize the American Manual Labor Institute. He also established a lumber mill and was awarded a bronze medal by Queen Victoria, in recognition of his decorative walnut cabinets which were displayed at the Crystal Palace Exhibit. In 1876, his second wife accompanied him to England, where he was presented with a gold-framed photograph of the queen. He was also received by the Archbishop of Canterbury and Prime Minister John Russell.

When Henson returned to the United States, he was received by President Rutherford B. Hayes. He died on May 5, 1883, at the age of 94, in Dresden, Ontario. His obituary appeared in the *New York Herald Tribune.* Whether hero or "Uncle Tom," Josiah Henson lived his life as best he could. And that, in the final analysis, is all that is required for any man to achieve greatness.

# JOHN JONES
## (1816-1879)

*Freeborn, John Jones was the leading Black Chicagoan of the 1800s, a philanthropist, and a well-known crusader against Illinois' "Black Laws." Jones was also the first Black elected official of Cook County; Underground Railroad station master; and founder of Jones Commercial School.*

John Jones was born in Greene County, North Carolina, on November 3, 1816, of a free Black mother and a German father. Fearing that his father might sell him into slavery, John's mother apprenticed him to a man named Sheppard, who taught John the tailoring trade. Sheppard later took John to Tennessee and hired him out to another tailor. His mother's fears echoed in his heart. Would he be sold into slavery?

In the mid-1800s in America, even free Blacks were continually at risk of being captured and sold. Jones suspected that he needed proof of his free status, so he petitioned the Tennessee courts for permission to return to his birthplace and obtain proof. Once there, he received the legal evidence he needed and persuaded Judge V. D. Barry to release him from his apprenticeship.

John returned to Memphis and worked there until 1841. He then moved to Alton, Illinois, where he married Mary Richardson. Seeking to better his position, John moved to Chicago with his wife and their only daughter, Lavinia. When the Jones family arrived, John could neither read nor write, and his entire savings consisted of $3.50. Nevertheless, John established a tailor shop and before long, he built a flourishing business that catered to the aristocracy of Chicago's "Gold Coast." By the time he was 30 years old, he had constructed a four-story building to house his business, and he was a wealthy, influential Chicagoan. In the meantime, as hard as he worked to increase his tailoring business, he still found time to teach himself to proficiently read and write.

Jones also found time to pursue and expand the civil rights activities which he began while in Alton. The Jones' home was an Underground Railroad station, and he hosted several abolitionists—including Frederick Douglass, John Brown, and Allan Pinkerton, who visited Jones before the Civil War. In addition to risking his luxurious life to aid fugitive slaves, Jones led a 12-year campaign to repeal the *Illinois Black Laws*. These laws denied free Blacks full citizenship: they required Blacks to carry documentation of their free status; a bond card indicating that they were well-behaved; they prohibited Blacks from testifying in court against Whites; and they denied Blacks the right to vote.

From 1853 to 1865, Jones used various means to get the laws repealed. In 1856, he went to the state capital to petition for Blacks rights. He took to the streets, asking anyone he met to support his fight for full civil rights. Then in 1864, he published a sixteen-page pamphlet, *The Black Laws of Illinois and A Few Reasons Why They Should Be Repealed.* In his pamphlet, Jones pointed out that he was paying taxes on more than $30,000 worth of property, yet he could not vote. Jones made speeches, wrote articles, and lobbied tirelessly until 1865, when the *Black Laws* were repealed.

Jones' business did not suffer while he promoted civil rights and abolitionist causes. Before the devastating 1871 Chicago Fire, his worth was estimated at $100,000—a handsome fortune in that day. True to his personality, though, Jones continued focusing on more than material gain. He was instrumental in lobbying for Illinois passage of the *Thirteenth, Fourteenth,* and *Fifteenth Amendments* to the U.S. Constitution. He also entered Illinois politics and became the first Black in Chicago to hold an elective office, when he served on the Cook County Board of Commissioners from 1871 to 1875.

When Jones died on May 21, 1879, he was eulogized by the *Chicago Tribune* as "the most prominent colored citizen in Chicago." With little more than his own energy and sense of duty to his people, John Jones rose from obscurity to national acclaim as a businessman, politician, and civil rights leader.

# WILLIAM C. NELL
## (1816-1874)

*William Nell was a Black history specialist, writer, journalist, and an antislavery agitator. A freeborn Bostonian, Nell graduated with honors from a racially mixed grammar school. However, he was denied an award for his scholastic achievements because of his color. This discriminatory treatment profoundly affected his lifelong campaign for equal treatment of Black students in Massachusetts' public schools.*

William C. Nell was born December 20, 1816, to William and Louisa Nell. His father served as a steward on a ship, the *General Gadsen,* but later settled in Boston where he became a tailor. Nell's father was also an associate of the militant Black abolitionist, David Walker.

In 1847, Nell organized the welcoming home ceremonies for Frederick Douglass, when the great freedom fighter returned to America after his triumphant European visit. Later that year, Nell was in attendance at the Colored Convention. Through his participation in the convention, he became close friends with William Lloyd Garrision and Frederick Douglass. Nell assisted both men in their journalistic ventures, primarily as a writer for Garrision's *Liberator* and Frederick Douglass' *North Star.* As the bond of friendship between Garrison and Nell grew, his relationship with Douglass waned. Douglass later charged that Nell had conspired against him, and the rift between the two men widened.

Nell, a vigorous writer, became interested in describing the Black man's contribution to the military. In 1851, he published a pamphlet, *Services for the Colored Americans in the Wars of 1776* and 1812. This pamphlet was later expanded and introduced with a preface by one of the great writers of the age, Wendell Phillips. *Services for the Colored Americans* was expanded to a full-scale study in 1855, with an introduction by Harriet Beecher Stowe. The expanded study not only detailed the Black man's military contributions, but it also highlighted other important aspects of the Black American's life and experiences in this country prior to 1850.

In addition to his journalistic endeavors, Nell vigorously campaigned to abolish Massachusetts' system of separate and unequal educational facilities for Black children. He pursued this for 15 years, beginning with the signing of a petition to the Massachusetts state legislature in 1840. However, it was not until April 1855 that the legislature voted to prohibit the exclusion of any child from any school because of race, color, or religion.

Not content with this major legal victory, Nell was also interested in the enforcement of the law. In September of the same year, Nell went from school to school to ensure that equal educational opportunity for Blacks was a reality. Because of this effort, both the Black and White abolitionist communities honored Nell in a ceremony attended by William Garrison, Wendell Phillips, Charles Remond, and other prominent citizens.

As an abolitionist, Nell contributed to the anti-slavery movement as a member of the racially mixed Vigilance Committee of Boston. He, and other prominent Black abolitionists, vigorously opposed both the American Colonization Society and the *Dred Scott* decision. The Society wanted Blacks to resettle in Africa. The *Dred Scott* decision, on the other hand, stripped Blacks of virtually all citizenship rights. Men like Nell, felt duty bound to oppose these racist, oppressive tactics.

Later in life, in 1861, Nell became the first Black person to be appointed to a federal position (postal clerk). He remained in this position until the time of his death, at age 58, on May 25, 1874. His good friend William Lloyd Garrison delivered his eulogy. Although he never achieved the fame of a Frederick Douglass or a Martin Delany, Nell's published works still serve as a valuable resource to historians today.

# ROBERT PURVIS
## (1810-1898)

*Freeborn, Robert was one of three sons of William Purvis, an Englishman and naturalized American citizen whose wealth was achieved in the cotton industry. Robert was unique among the Black abolitionists because of the great wealth he inherited from his father.*

Robert Purvis was born on August 4, 1810, in South Carolina. His grandmother, Dido Badaraka, was a Moroccan slave who was kidnapped as a child and sold into slavery. At age 19, she was granted her freedom and later married a German, Baron Judah. Their daughter, Harriet, married an Englishman, William Purvis, Robert's father.

When he was 9 years old, Robert was sent to Philadelphia and enrolled in a private school. His father helped him understand the anti-slavery issues and provided him with books on the subject. When William Purvis died in 1826, he left Robert what was then a fortune, $120,000. Robert later attended Amherst College. In spite of his inherited wealth and the possibility of a life of ease, he chose instead to join the battle for the abolition of slavery and to promote justice for Blacks in America.

As an Underground Railroad agent, Purvis hid fugitive slaves in a secret room he had constructed, which could only be entered through a well-concealed trap door. Robert and his wife, Harriet, frequently played host to abolitionist leaders as well as runaway slaves. His home soon came to be known among the abolitionists as "Saints' Rest," where "the wicked ceased from troubling and the weary are at rest."

Purvis also dedicated himself to the economic advancement of Black people. In 1831, he supported efforts to establish a training school for Black students. Two years later, Purvis joined William Lloyd Garrison in organizing the American Anti-Slavery Society. In 1833, Purvis also co-founded the Philadelphia Library Company of Colored Persons, and he also opposed legislation designed to stop out-of-state free Blacks from settling in Pennsylvania. And, he fought the implementation of a new state constitution that would prevent Blacks from voting.

From 1845 to 1850, Purvis served as president of the Pennsylvania Anti-Slavery Society. He also served as chairman of the General Vigilance Committee, an arm of the Underground Railroad, for a comparable period of time. And in 1853, Purvis refused to pay his taxes when Black students were excluded from the public schools in Byberry, Pennsylvania. As a Garrisonian, in May 1857, Purvis publicly attacked the United States government as "one of the baddest, meanest, most atrocious [examples of] despotism that ever saw the face of the Sun."

After the Civil War, Purvis spent less time with abolitionist activity and more time at home. He tended his beautiful, tree-lined lawn, his fruit orchard, and his prized livestock. On December 4, 1883, he attended the fiftieth anniversary of the American Anti-Slavery Society, where he was reunited with two of the other founders, Elizur Wright, Jr. and the great American poet, John Greenleaf Whittier.

Purvis' other great joy in life was the growth and development of his son, Charles. Steeped in anti-slavery thought by both parents, Charles grew to become a leader. Since Charles' mother was the daughter of James Forten, and one of the co-founders of the Philadelphia Female Anti-Slavery Society, it was a source of great pride to Robert that his son, who later became surgeon-in-chief at Freedmen's Hospital in Washington, D.C., would carry on the Purvis tradition of generosity, commitment, and achievement.

Robert Purvis died on April 15, 1898, of apoplexy. He was survived by his son, Charles, and a second wife. He was eulogized in the *New York Times* and the *Washington Bee*. Also, the American Negro Historical Society registered its praise of this great hero in Black American history.

# CHARLES L. REMOND
## (1810-1873)

*Charles Lenox Remond was a freeborn mulatto born in Salem, Massachusetts, on February 1, 1810, to John and Nancy Remond. He was provided with an excellent education in the public schools of Salem, along with his equally famous sister, Sarah Parker Remond. In the decline of his life, Charles was forced to open a ladies and men's dining room to supplement his income. He also served as a recruiter in the Civil War.*

In the two decades prior to the Civil War, anti-slavery activity reached a fever pitch. Prior to 1840, the anti-slavery movement was dominated by White men such as William Lloyd Garrison and the uncompromising John Brown. These men and others, including many Quakers, had been the chief spokesmen opposing slavery on legal, moral, and political grounds.

However, David Walker's appeal for all-out war against slaveholders, the raid at Harper's Ferry, and a series of repressive legal actions further fueled the anti-slavery movement. In the process, it increased the demand for Black men to step forward to articulate the horrors of slavery and the injustice of this "peculiar institution." Charles Remond was the first of a series of Black abolitionists who were in demand as lecturers. After Remond, came such greats as Samuel Ringgold Ward, Henry Highland Garnet, and later, the greatest orator of them all, Frederick Augustus Douglass. But it was Charles L. Remond who set the stage with his skillful oratory.

In 1838, Remond was appointed a lecturing agent of the Massachusetts Anti-Slavery Society. In this role, he canvassed the states of New York, Massachusetts, Pennsylvania, Rhode Island, and Maine. Two years later, he represented the American Anti-Slavery Society at the World's Anti-Slavery Society Convention in England. Wherever he traveled in Europe, he was enthusiastically received.

When Remond returned, he brought with him an "Address from the People of Ireland," which contained 60,000 signatures urging Irish Americans to oppose slavery and support liberty and justice for all men regardless of race. During this period, Remond was probably the most famous Black man in America.

In 1842, Remond became the first Black American to address the legislative committee of the Massachusetts House of Representatives. He stated; "Mr. Chairman, the treatment to which colored Americans are exposed in their own country finds a counterpart in no other; and I am free to declare that, in the course of 19 months traveling in England, Ireland, and Scotland, I was received, treated and recognized in public and private society without regard to my complexion."

Remond's more radical side appeared when, in 1855, he spoke at a meeting honoring William C. Nell for his efforts in desegregating Boston's public schools. At this meeting, he urged Blacks to withhold their taxes if they were not receiving the benefits intended to be derived from taxation. "No privilege, no pay," was his very succinct way of stating one of the principles on which America was founded.

Unfortunately, Remond suffered chronic ill health. In addition, the income from his anti-slavery lectures was spotty, at best. He also became somewhat disenchanted with certain aspects of the anti-slavery movement, and his philosophical position was at odds with Frederick Douglass. By that time, Douglass had totally eclipsed Remond as a favored lecturer and, through this combination of circumstances, Remond's star began to fade.

Remond was married twice, and he and his second wife, Elizabeth Thayer Magee, produced several children who later died in their childhood. Elizabeth died in 1872. Sick from the tuberculosis which afflicted his entire family, and somewhat disillusioned, Charles Lenox Remond died on December 22, 1873, at the age of 63.

# SARAH P. REMOND
## (1826-1894)

*Sarah Parker Remond, abolitionist, physician, and sister of Charles Lenox Remond, was born in Salem, Massachusetts to John and Nancy Remond in 1826. Her father was a native of the island of Curacao and on May 2, 1811, he received his United States citizenship.*

Compared to the life of the slaves, Sarah lived a life of elegance and leisure. One historical source described her as "...well-bred, well-educated, well-clothed, and well-housed." During the mid-1850s, she lived with her brother and his wife. The Remond household was the center of anti-slavery and intellectual activities, and was frequented by William L. Garrison, Wendell Phillips, John Greenleaf Whittier, and William Wells Brown. Also, the renowned abolitionist Charlotte Forten lived with the Remonds while she attended school in Salem. Sarah Remond served as a model and heroine to the younger Charlotte.

Sarah became one of the leading speakers of the abolitionist movement. She began to give lectures in 1842, often joining her brother at the podium, in their mutual quest to dismantle the pillars of slavery. Sarah was considered a gifted and zealous advocate of the cause of her oppressed race.

In 1853, Sarah Remond won a discrimination lawsuit and was awarded $500 in damages because she was forcibly removed from her seat, at a theatrical performance in Boston. In 1856, she and her brother, Charles, addressed the anti-slavery conventions in New York and Canada. Several times during her tours, she was subjected to stinging racial insults and she was denied hotel accommodations because of her color.

Like her brother and many other leading abolitionists, Sarah's campaign trail to combat slavery and discrimination transcended international boundaries. In 1858, tired of the discrimination that she had experienced while lecturing in the United States, Sarah decided to travel to England to "breathe free air" and "to further her education," as one source put it. She lectured in England, Scotland, and Ireland, where she addressed eminent statesmen, clergymen, professors, philosophers, scientists, and other distinguished persons.

Sarah arrived in London in 1859, where her forceful presence stimulated the formation of the London Emancipation Committee. During her stay in England, she was presented with a gold watch as a symbol of respect and admiration. The watch was inscribed; "Presented to S. P. Remond by English women, her sisters, in Warrington, February 2nd, 1859." For two years, from October 1859 to 1861, she attended the Bedford College for Ladies which later became part of the University of London. In 1864, the Ladies London Emancipation Society published Sarah Remond's pamphlet, *The Negroes and Anglo-Africans as Freedmen and Soldiers.*

Upon her return to the United States in 1866, Sarah Remond, her brother, and Frederick Douglass campaigned for equal political rights for emancipated Blacks. She returned to England again that year to attend a celebration in honor of William Lloyd Garrison. Later that year, Sarah moved to Florence, Italy, where she attended the school of the Santa Maria Nuova Hospital between 1866 and 1868. After obtaining a medical certificate, she practiced medicine in Florence. She never returned to the United States.

On April 25, 1877, Sarah married Lazzaro Pintor. Years later, Sarah P. Remond died in Rome on December 13, 1894, at the age of 68. She, like thousands of other Blacks, had made a new life for herself in another country. But before she moved to Italy, Sarah Remond dedicated many years to the energetic advocacy of equal rights for her people.

# DAVID RUGGLES
## (1810-1849)

*David Ruggles was a gifted speaker and writer who possessed great intellect. Born to Nancy and David Ruggles, Sr., in Norwich, Connecticut, in 1810, he was the eldest child. As a freeborn Black, he was able to get a basic education at the Sabbath School for the Poor in Norwich. The Sabbath Schools admitted Blacks and offered religious and moral instruction, as well as the rudiments of reading, writing, and arithmetic.*

At age 17, David moved to New York. By 1829, he opened a grocery store and became involved in the abolitionist fervor of that city. In 1833, he became a traveling agent for the *Emancipator and Journal of Public Morals,* a popular anti-slavery publication. In 1834, he opened a bookstore and distributed anti-slavery and anti-colonization literature. His bookstore may well have been the first ever owned by a Black man in America.

From 1835 to 1838, Ruggles also became active in the Underground Railroad movement. He assisted William Still and, like this great abolitionist leader, is credited with helping over 600 fugitive slaves escape to freedom. One of the most notable runaways he assisted was Frederick Douglass, whom he befriended. He housed Douglass when he first fled to New York, and he helped Douglass in his plans to marry Anna Murray. As a result of his tireless efforts, Ruggles became known as the "Father of the Underground Railroad."

Ruggles later served as secretary to the New York Vigilance Committee. During the committee's first year, he personally handled well over 300 cases dealing with Blacks' rights and fugitive slaves. Judged to be one of the best writers of the era, Ruggles used his journalistic skills to mount persuasive arguments against colonization and slavery. He was described as a "critical, witty, and logical writer."

Aside from producing many pamphlets, from 1838 to 1841, Ruggles edited and published *Mirror of Liberty.* This magazine was first published as a quarterly and later as a weekly.

It advocated the rights of Blacks and bitterly opposed the political and legal demands of the slaveholding South.

Tragically, blindness and ill health cut short Ruggles' career as an anti-slavery activist. When prescribed medical treatment failed him, Ruggles developed his own method of treatment, which included proper diet, rest, and hydrotherapy. After 18 months of self-treatment, Ruggles regained much of his eyesight and overall health. The news of his remarkable recovery spread to others, and soon he found himself treating patients with his technique. In the process of treating his many patients, Ruggles discovered and developed the theory of "cutaneous electricity," which was based on his belief that the skin is "the organ through which the symptoms and characters of diseases" were indicated. His theory has been supported by medical specialists throughout the ages.

In 1846, Ruggles opened one of the first hydropathic centers in the United States. Among the many persons who came to him seeking relief was Sojourner Truth, who he successfully treated and cured of scrofulous humors (swollen lymph glands) and dyspepsia. William Lloyd Garrison was another of his more famous patients. From 1846 to 1849, Ruggles' hydropathic institute flourished in Northampton, Massachusetts, where he owned or leased 112 acres and several buildings for the institute.

Those who knew him described Ruggles as a man "of ordinary size, with an athletic form and dark complexion." It was also noted that he had "a benevolent and intelligent countenance." This unusual man worked relentlessly to help others, whether through his practice of hydropathy, or through his extensive abolitionist activity.

David Ruggles died on December 26, 1849, at age thirty-nine, of an intestinal disorder. Although his life was shortened by illness, his contributions to the Underground Railroad became legendary, and his writings equalled or surpassed those of Frederick Douglass.

# MARIA W. STEWART
## (1803-1879)

*Maria W. Miller Stewart is generally acknowledged as the first American-born woman to lecture in public. She is best known for speeches that addressed issues of Black economic advancement, the abolition of slavery, and African pride. Although her speeches addressed worldly matters, she typically spoke in biblical tones. She made her first speech in Boston, in 1832.*

Maria Stewart was born in Hartford, Connecticut, in 1803. Her parents died when she was 5 years old, and from the time of their death until she was about 15, she was indentured to a local clergyman and his family. Her parents were freeborn Blacks and little else is known about them. Maria had very little formal education.

On August 10, 1826, Maria married James W. Stewart, a veteran of the War of 1812. Three years after the marriage, Stewart died. Unscrupulous lawyers cheated Maria out of the inheritance her husband had provided, leaving her destitute. In 1830, it is reported that she made a public profession of "faith in Christ," and dedicated her life to His service. In spite of her poor education, she was able to write essays which were printed in pamphlet form by the White abolitionist, William Lloyd Garrison. The publication of her work generated a small income for Maria.

When Maria Stewart began to lecture publicly, such activity was virtually unheard of for women. The nineteenth century's society offered few employment opportunities for women, for it was viewed that a woman's place was in the home. In 1837, two White women, Sarah and Angelina Grimke, were the first of their race to publicly lecture and join the anti-slavery circuit. Maria began her public speaking five years earlier.

In her speeches, Stewart challenged the *"daughters of Africa"* to use their resources to uplift the Black race. She asked, "Why cannot we do something to distinguish ourselves and contribute some of our hard earnings that would reflect honor upon our memories and cause our children to arise and call us blessed?" She appealed to Black women to build their own schools and stores, stating; "Charity begins at home, and those that provide not for their own are worse than infidels." She summoned Black men to petition Congress to abolish slavery and to grant Black people equal rights.

Stewart's speeches made her few friends in Boston. At the time, it was considered promiscuous for a woman to be engaged in this type of activity. Stewart responded to her Black critics by noting that both God and St. Paul had spoken through women. However, the harsh criticism continued. Hurt and disillusioned, on September 21, 1833, Maria Stewart decided to leave Boston, "For I find it is no use for me, as an individual, to try to make myself useful among my color in this city."

Stewart moved to New York, where she continued her education by joining the Female Literary Society. She later became a teacher and taught school in Manhattan, Brooklyn, and Washington, D.C. In 1871, with money she saved, Stewart opened a Sabbath School near Howard University in Washington, D.C. She barely kept a roof over her head, and she appealed to Black community leaders for help. They hosted a fundraiser for her, then duped her out of most of the proceeds.

The loss of her husband and his inheritance, the harsh criticism in Boston, and the treatment of her own people, made Stewart very despondent. Still, she persevered. In 1879, she successfully obtained her husband's pension. She used the funds to publish the second edition of her speeches and writings, *Meditations from the Pen of Mrs. Maria W. Stewart.*

To the end, always a proud woman, Maria Stewart died, at age 76, in the Freedmens Hospital in Washington, D.C., in 1879.

# WILLIAM L. STILL
## (1821-1902)

*The Fugitive Slave Act of 1850 gave great powers to southern slaveholders seeking to recapture their runaway slaves. This oppressive legislation had an impact quite the opposite of its intent. It fanned abolitionist sentiment and increased northern sympathy for the plight of Blacks in slavery. Additionally, the Act boosted traffic on the Underground Railroad.*

One of the Underground Railroad's most remarkable conductors was William Lloyd Still. Under threat of severe penalty if he were caught, Still heroically assisted 649 Black men, women, and children in their journey from slavery to freedom. His book, *The Underground Railroad*, published in 1872, is a priceless record of the life and death struggles of hundreds of runaway slaves. The book provided perhaps the best and most accurate documentation of the Underground Railroad. However, given the need for secrecy in aiding runaways, what prompted Still to keep such records?

Perhaps the answer lies in one of Still's most dramatic experiences as an Underground Railroad agent. One day in August 1850, a young runaway slave, named Peter, told Still he was looking for his parents. As the man detailed his story, Still stood mesmerized. Peter was looking for Levin and Sidney Steel. Actually, Peter was an older brother whom William had never met! He later reported that this incident inspired him to keep records of runaway slaves in the hope that this might enable them to find loved ones.

Still was the youngest of 18 children born to Levin and Sidney Steel. His mother, Levin, had been forced to leave Peter in bondage during her escape from slavery. Levin and Sidney changed their name from "Steel" to "Still" in order to disguise their identity. Born in 1821, William spent most of his younger years working on his father's farm in New Jersey. He left New Jersey in 1844, and eventually settled in Philadelphia, Pennsylvania.

When Still arrived in Philadelphia he was an illiterate farm boy. Within three years, he had taught himself to read and write. In 1847, he married Letitia George, who made him the proud father of four children. That same year, Still landed a job as a clerk with the Pennsylvania Anti-Slavery Society. Although merely a clerk, Still immediately became involved in the broader activities of the Anti-Slavery Society.

As a result of the *Fugitive Slave Act*, Philadelphia's White abolitionist community organized a vigilance committee. This committee's purpose was to assist the increasingly large numbers of fugitive slaves who were passing through Philadelphia. Still was named chairman of the committee.

After the Civil War, Still devoted his time to combatting racism and discrimination. His efforts had begun as early as 1859, when he started a campaign to stop racial discrimination on Philadelphia's railroad cars by exposing the practice in the press. Also, in 1861, he helped organize a social, civil, and statistical association to collect and preserve information about Black Americans.

Later in life, William Still became active in philanthropic and business efforts. In 1880, he organized one of the first YMCAs for Black youth; served on the Freedmen's Aid Commission; and as a result of his success as a businessman, became a member of the Philadelphia Board of Trade. Still's success in business resulted from a thriving stove and coal business, which he established during the Civil War.

William Still died in Philadelphia in 1902, at the age of 81. This once illiterate farm boy, through his innate intelligence, dedication, and hard work, became one of the leading citizens of Philadelphia. Without question, he is one of the great heroes of Black American history.

# NAT TURNER
## (1800-1831)

*At about 2 a.m. on Monday, August 22, 1831, six rebel slaves began one of the most sensational insurrections of the slave era. Nat Turner, the "Black Prophet" led the attack, beginning at the home of his master, Joseph Travis.*

Nat Turner, the property of Benjamin Turner, was born of slave parents in Southampton County, Virginia, in 1800. In his early manhood, he worked as a field hand in the production of cotton and tobacco. He was also mechanically gifted and deeply religious.

With his brilliant mind, Turner taught himself to read and was later able to quote long passages from the Bible. The "Black Prophet," as he became known, also acquired an ample knowledge of science and mechanics to make his various masters, four in all, proud to own him. Turner was also intensely loyal. Even though he had escaped from slavery in 1821, after six weeks in hiding, a sense of religious duty caused him to return.

In 1828, Nat had a vision telling him that it was his God-given duty to struggle against the enslavement of his people. When, in February 1831, a solar eclipse occurred, the deeply religious Turner took it as another "sign" that he should instigate an open rebellion against slavery. At the time, many newspapers reported that this eclipse had a marked effect on many people in the United States. For six months, Turner carefully laid out the plans of his insurrection.

On August 22, 1831, Turner and six other slaves began their uprising at the home of his master, Joseph Travis. There, five people were killed—three men, a woman, and a child. Several hours later, the six rebels were joined by more than 70 other slaves. For 40 hours, with many on horseback, they ravaged Southampton County, Virginia. However, the killing of Whites was not indiscriminate. Many Whites, who were no better off than the slaves, were spared.

News of the Turner rebellion sprouted like wildfire throughout the South. As a result, many other uprisings and plots, and reported plots, occurred immediately. This was true in virtually every slave state, especially Virginia and North Carolina. Thousands of slaves were arrested and many executed in the South until early 1833.

Turner's initial plan was to terrorize the countryside and capture the local county seat (the town of Jerusalem), but he and his band of rebels never made it to the county seat, where they had hoped to get fresh arms and ammunition. Instead, they were subdued by hundreds of state militamen, volunteer military companies, and police.

Thirteen of the insurrectionists were hanged immediately and others were arrested, tried, and later executed. But Turner and a handful of comrades managed to escape, where upon a $500 reward was offered, by Governor John Floyd of Virginia, for Turner's capture. His presence was reported many times in various parts of the county, when actually he was hiding out in a cave in Southampton. While he was being sought, his wife was often harassed and beaten. However, Turner was captured in Southampton on October 30, 1831.

November 5, 1831, was Nat Turner's day of reckoning. At his trial, he claimed no feelings of guilt for his actions. An interrogator stated that when he tried to get him to admit to what he had done was wrong and foolish, Turner responded; "Was not Christ crucified?" The verdict? "[You will] be hung by the neck until you are dead! dead! dead!" Six days later, Nat went calmly to his death.

Nat Turner's courageous stand, his proud defiance to the bitter end, and the fiercely unjust attacks on innocent Blacks following the rebellion, all served to hasten the day when slavery in America would be brought to an end.

# DAVID WALKER
## (1785-1830)

*Free born, David Walker was no ordinary man. His imposing looks and absolute intolerance of slavery characterized him as one of the most dynamic of the Black abolitionists. Walker was the first Black man to attack slavery through the press.*

David Walker was born in 1785, in Wilmington, North Carolina, the son of a slave father and a freeborn Black woman. Since his mother was free, David was also free, in spite of the fact that he lived in the slaveholding South. Although details of his life in the South are sketchy, it is known that he traveled widely from plantation to plantation and witnessed firsthand the evils of slavery. When he reached his 30s, Walker had experienced enough of the Deep South.

In 1825, Walker settled in Boston, Massachusetts, where two years later he opened a successful secondhand clothing store. He also taught himself to read and write. Once having achieved these skills, he began to study in order to quench his relentless thirst for knowledge and understanding. He studied the history of the slave systems in Egypt, Greece, Rome, Africa, Asia, and America. He also studied the framing of the *Declaration of Independence.*

Walker's surveyed conclusion was that while Africans had some White friends in England and America, however, the vast majority of Whites were the "natural enemies" of Blacks and people of color. He further concluded that Blacks worldwide had the numbers and power to alter their destiny, and they should rise up against their oppressors.

While operating his very successful clothing store on Boston's Brattle Street, Walker began to speak and write forcefully on the subject of ending slavery. Had he concentrated on his thriving business, he might have become a wealthy man. Instead, Walker used his money to help others and eventually, to publish the most powerful piece of anti-slavery literature of its time: *David Walker's Appeal in four articles together with a Preamble to the Colored Citizens of the World, but in particular and very expressly, to those in the United States of America.*

Walker's *Appeal*, which appeared in 1829, was a 76 page thunderbolt which struck terror in the slaveholding South, shook up northern abolitionists, and helped to rouse free Blacks from their conciliatory approach to slavery and injustice. The document broke conventional theories of gradualism and established a revolutionary conception of Pan- Africanism and open Black rebellion. Walker wrote: "... had you not rather be killed than to be a slave to a tyrant, who takes the life of your mother, wife, and dear little children?"

The *Appeal* was widely read by free Blacks and Whites. However, southern legislators, fearing inflammatory disobedience and uprisings, banned the book and enacted laws forbidding Blacks to read and write. Abolitionists who favored gradual, peaceful means for Black emancipation, denounced the work, and many free Blacks considered it too radical. A group of Georgia slaveholders even placed a bounty on Walker's head; $1,000 dead, or $10,000 alive.

Following David Walker's mysterious death in 1830, Henry Highland Garnet wrote that he had been "hurried out of life by means of poison." Walker's *Appeal*, however, continued to have profound impact on the direction of the anti-slavery movement. It is believed, for example, that Nat Turner was highly influenced by the *Appeal*.

After Walker's death, his wife, Eliza, gave birth to a son. His son, Edwin, became the first Black elected to the Massachusetts legislature. In the *Appeal*, as well as in his son, David Walker's spirit lived on!

# REV. SAMUEL RINGGOLD WARD
## (1817-1866)

*Samuel R. Ward was of pure African ancestry, whose color was referred to "as black as coal." Ward was known by his abolitionist contemporaries as the "Black Daniel Webster." He was a pastor, teacher, commanding orator, Underground Railroad conductor, and much more.*

Ward was born into slavery on October 17, 1817, to William and Anne Ward, on the eastern shore of Maryland. When Samuel was about 3 years old, his family fled to New Jersey and finally escaped to New York City, which Ward commonly referred to as "this city of ever crushing Negro hate." While in New York, he attended the African Free School, along with fellow students Henry Highland Garnet and Alexander Crummel. He also briefly attended Oneida Theological Institute.

In 1839, Ward was licensed to preach by the New York Congregationalist Association. Also that year, Ward met Gerrit Smith, a White abolitionist, who sponsored him in much the same manner as Garrison sponsored and promoted Frederick Douglass in his earlier days. His pastorates of two White churches, from 1841 to 1851, were propagandized by Black abolitionists to refute pro-slavery activists' theories regarding the inferiority of the Black man.

Ward was ranked by many anti-slavery activists as one of the most skilled lecturers of his time. He served as a lecturing agent for the American and Canadian Anti-Slavery Societies, and his rhetorical skills were rated, by many leading authorities, second only to Frederick Douglass and Charles L. Remond. Frederick Douglass once stated of Ward; "No colored man who has yet attracted public attention in this country, was ever capable of rendering his people greater service than he."

In addition to being an outstanding orator, Ward supported the Liberty party and two journalistic efforts. His first newspaper, the *Imperial Citizen*, was published in 1848. The second paper was called the *Northern Star and Colored Farmer*. Both papers were published in Syracuse, New York.

In 1851, Ward aided a fugitive slave, named Jerry, and fearing that he might be apprehended, he fled to Canada and declared himself a British subject. While in Canada, he resided in Toronto and lent his energies to support many efforts to assist Black refugees in the area. Ward helped establish refugee settlements, and he continued to speak out against all instances of racial prejudice in Canada. He also continued his work as a newspaperman; in 1853, Ward founded *Provincial Freeman*, a newspaper that continued publication until 1857.

In 1853, Ward traveled to Europe to help raise funds for the Anti-Slavery Society of Canada. His *Autobiography of the Fugitive Negro: His Anti-Slavery Labours in the United States, Canada, and England* was published in 1855, while he was in England. The first section of his book briefly sketched his life, and the remaining portion addressed anti-slavery issues and provided an extensive sociological study of Blacks in America.

In 1855, Ward was given 50 acres of land in Jamaica by an English Quaker, John Chandler. Ward then decided to move to Kingston, Jamaica, where he became pastor of a small Baptist congregation. In 1860, he moved to St. George Parish and became unsuccessfully involved in a series of unproductive projects. It is reported that Samuel Ward, the once outstanding orator, died in poverty in Jamaica, in 1866.

# Excerpts from Frederick Douglass' Independence Day Address
## July 5, 1852
### Rochester, New York

Fellow-citizens, pardon me, allow me to ask, why am I called upon to speak here to-day? What have I, or those I represent, to do with your national independence? Are the great principles of political freedom and of natural justice, embodied in that Declaration of Independence, extended to us? And am I, therefore called upon to bring our humble offering to the national altar, and to confess the benefits and express devout gratitude for the blessings resulting from your independence to us?

This Fourth July is *yours*, not *mine*. You may rejoice, I must mourn. To drag a man in fetters into the grand illuminated temple of liberty, and call upon him to join you in joyous anthems, were inhuman mockery and sacrilegious irony. Do you mean, citizens, to mock me, by asking me to speak today? If so, there is a parallel to your conduct. And let me warn you that it is dangerous to copy the example of a nation whose crimes, towering up to heaven, were thrown down by the breath of the Almighty, burying that nation in irrevocable ruin! I can to-day take up the plaintive lament of a peeled and woe-smitten people!

Fellow-citizens, above your national, tumultuous joy, I hear the mournful wail of millions! whose chains, heavy and grievous yesterday, are, today, rendered more intolerable by the jubilee shouts that reach them. If I do forget, if I do not faithfully remember those bleeding children of sorrow this day, "may my right hand forget her cunning, and may my tongue cleave to the roof of my mouth!" To forget them, to pass lightly over their wrongs, and to chime in with the popular theme, would be treason most scandalous and shocking, and would make me a reproach before God and the world. My subject, then, fellow-citizens, is AMERICAN SLAVERY. I shall see this day and its popular characteristics from the slave's point of view. Standing there identified with the American bondman, making his wrongs mine, I do not hesitate to declare, with all my soul, that the character and conduct of this nation never looked blacker to me than on this 4th of July! Whether we turn to the declarations of the past, or to the professions of the present, the conduct of the nation seems equally hideous and revolting. America is false to the past, false to the present, and solemnly binds herself to be false to the future.

What, am I to argue that it is wrong to make men brutes, to rob them of their liberty, to work them without wages, to keep them ignorant of their relations to their fellow men, to beat them with sticks, to flay their flesh with the lash, to load their limbs with irons, to hunt them with dogs, to sell them at auction, to sunder their families, to knock out their teeth, to burn their flesh, to starve them into obedience and submission to their masters? Must I argue that a system thus marked with blood, and stained with pollution, is wrong? No! I will not. I have better employment for my time and strength than such arguments would imply.

Go where you may, search where you will, roam through all the monarchies and despotisms of the Old World, travel through South America, search out every abuse, and when you have found the last, lay your facts by the side of the ever-day practices of this nation, and you will say with me, that, for revolting barbarity and shameless hypocrisy, America reigns without a rival . . . .

*Frederick Douglass*

# TEST YOURSELF

Now that you have familiarized yourself with our historic Black Abolitionists, in this fifth series of Empak's Black History publications, this section, in three parts: MATCH; TRUE/FALSE; MULTIPLE CHOICE/FILL-IN, is designed to help you remember some key points about each notable Black Abolitionist. (Answers on page 32)

## MATCH

I. *Match the column on the right with the column on the left by placing the appropriate alphabetical letter next to the Abolitionist it represents.*

1. David Ruggles _____
2. Maria Stewart _____
3. Prince Hall _____
4. Samuel Ward _____
5. Nat Turner _____
6. David Walker _____
7. Josiah Henson _____
8. William Still _____

A) Wrote the *Appeal*
B) Masonic founder and official
C) "Father of the Underground Railroad"
D) Model for *Uncle Tom's Cabin*
E) First female Abolitionist speaker
F) Wrote *The Underground Railroad*
G) "Black Daniel Webster"
H) "Black Prophet"

## TRUE/FALSE

II. *The True and False statements below are taken from the biographical information given on each of the Abolitionists.*

1. Frederick Douglass was the grandson of a Mandingo prince. _____
2. John Jones was born in Chicago. _____
3. Richard Allen founded the AME church. _____
4. Charles and Sarah Remond were husband and wife. _____
5. Charlotte Forten was a published poet. _____
6. Henry Garnet called for a slave revolt. _____
7. Robert Purvis was one of Pennsylvania's key Abolitionists. _____
8. Martin Delany attended Princeton University. _____

## MULTIPLE CHOICE/FILL-IN

III. *Complete the statements below by underlining the correct name, or by filling-in the correct answer which you have read in the biographical sketches.*

1. Alexander Crummel lived in _____ for over twenty years.
2. (Martin Delany, Maria Stewart, Henry Bibb) had six masters and attempted to escape six times.
3. (Samuel Ward, Nat Turner, David Walker) was the Abolitionist promoted to refute racists' theories of Black inferiority.
4. _____ wrote *Clotel, or The President's Daughter.*
5. One of America's first hydropathists was _____.
6. (Frederick Douglass, John Jones, Richard Allen) became the first AME bishop.
7. The home of _____ was known as "Saints' Rest."

# CROSSWORD PUZZLE

ACROSS

1. Founded Canada's first Black newspaper
3. Chicago Abolitionist
9. Graduated from Queen's College in Cambridge
16. Organized slave revolt
18. Last name of author of military study
19. Last name of radical clothing store owner
20. First Black Abolitionist in demand as lecturer
21. Last name of Abolitionist who became a doctor in Italy
22. Survivor of raid at Harper's Ferry
23. Aided Douglass with his escape

DOWN

1. Addressed the U.S. House of Representatives
2. Founded the AME church
3. Fought in Canadian Rebellion of 1837-1838
4. Pastor of two White churches
5. First name of 18 across and 15 down
6. First name of 21 across
7. Attended Harvard Medical School
8. Prominent Mason
10. First name of 19 across
11. Her grandfather and father were Abolitionists
12. First woman public speaker
13. Founded *North Star* newspaper
14. Author of *The Underground Railroad*
15. Middle and last names of first Black American to publish a novel
17. Inherited $120,000

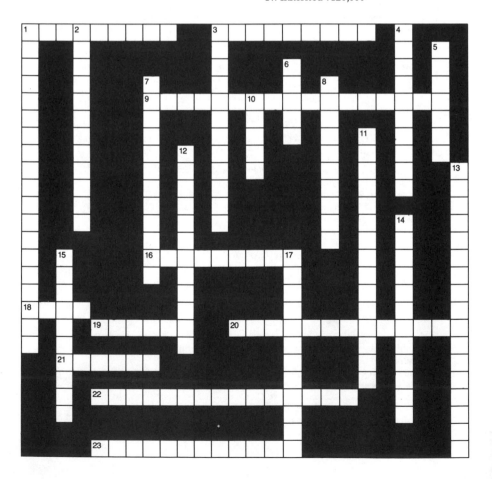

# WORDSEARCH

1. Richard Allen
2. Osborne Anderson
3. Henry Bibb
4. William Brown
5. Alexander Crummell
6. Martin Delany
7. Frederick Douglass
8. Charlotte Forten
9. Henry Garnet
10. Prince Hall
11. Josiah Henson
12. John Jones
13. William Nell
14. Robert Purvis
15. Charles Remond
16. Sarah Remond
17. David Ruggles
18. Maria Stewart
19. William Still
20. Nat Turner
21. David Walker
22. Samuel Ward

The names of our twenty-two HISTORIC BLACK ABOLITIONISTS are contained in the diagram below. Look in the diagram of letters for the names given in the list. Find the names by reading FORWARD, BACKWARDS, UP, DOWN, and DIAGONALLY in a straight line of letters. Each time you find a name in the diagram, circle it in the diagram and cross it off on the list of names. Words often overlap, and letters may be used more than once.

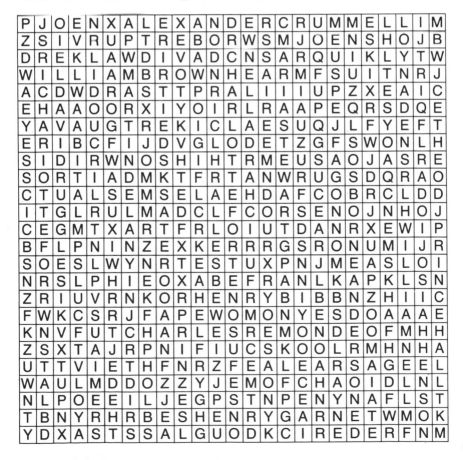

## MATCH

| | |
|---|---|
| 1.–C | 5.–H |
| 2.–E | 6.–A |
| 3.–B | 7.–D |
| 4.–G | 8.–F |

## TRUE/FALSE

| | |
|---|---|
| 1.–FALSE | 5.–TRUE |
| 2.–FALSE | 6.–TRUE |
| 3.–TRUE | 7.–TRUE |
| 4.–FALSE | 8.–FALSE |

## MULTIPLE CHOICE

1.–LIBERIA
2.–HENRY BIBB
3.–SAMUEL WARD
4.–WILLIAM WELLS BROWN

5.–DAVID RUGGLES
6.–RICHARD ALLEN
7.–ROBERT PURVIS

## CROSSWORD PUZZLE

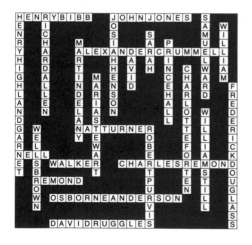

## WORD SEARCH

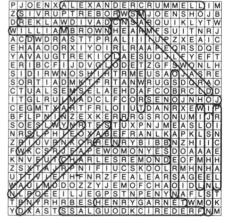

Name _____

Affiliation _____

Address _____
P. O. Box numbers not accepted, street address must appear.

City _____ State _____ Zip _____

Phone# (_____)_____ Date _____

Method Of Payment Enclosed:　　( ) Check　　　　( ) Money Order　　　　( ) Purchase Order

### Prices effective 11/1/95 thru 10/31/96

## ADVANCED LEVEL

| Quantity | ISBN # | Title Description | Unit Price | Total Price |
|---|---|---|---|---|
| | 0-922162-1-8 | "A Salute to Historic Black Women" | | |
| | 0-922162-2-6 | "A Salute to Black Scientists & Inventors" | | |
| | 0-922162-3-4 | "A Salute to Black Pioneers" | | |
| | 0-922162-4-2 | "A Salute to Black Civil Rights Leaders" | | |
| | 0-922162-5-0 | "A Salute to Historic Black Abolitionists" | | |
| | 0-922162-6-9 | "A Salute to Historic African Kings & Queens" | | |
| | 0-922162-7-7 | "A Salute to Historic Black Firsts" | | |
| | 0-922162-8-5 | "A Salute to Historic Blacks in the Arts" | | |
| | 0-922162-9-3 | "A Salute to Blacks in the Federal Government" | | |
| | 0-922162-14-X | "A Salute to Historic Black Educators" | | |

## INTERMEDIATE LEVEL

| Quantity | ISBN # | Title Description | Unit Price | Total Price |
|---|---|---|---|---|
| | 0-922162-75-1 | "Historic Black Women" | | |
| | 0-922162-76-X | "Black Scientists & Inventors" | | |
| | 0-922162-77-8 | "Historic Black Pioneers" | | |
| | 0-922162-78-6 | "Black Civil Rights Leaders" | | |
| | 0-922162-80-8 | "Historic Black Abolitionists" | | |
| | 0-922162-81-6 | "Historic African Kings & Queens" | | |
| | 0-922162-82-4 | "Historic Black Firsts" | | |
| | 0-922162-83-2 | "Historic Blacks in the Arts" | | |
| | 0-922162-84-0 | "Blacks in the Federal Government" | | |
| | 0-922162-85-9 | "Historic Black Educators" | | |

| Total Books | | ❸ Subtotal | |
|---|---|---|---|
| | | ❹ IL Residents add 8.75% Sales Tax | |
| SEE ABOVE CHART ⟶ | | ❺ Shipping & Handling | |
| GRADE LEVEL: 4th, 5th, 6th | | ❻ Total | |

### BOOK PRICING ● QUANTITY DISCOUNTS

| Advanced Level | Intermediate Level |
|---|---|
| Reg. $3.49 | Reg. $2.29 |
| Order 50 or More | Order 50 or More |
| Save 40¢ EACH | Save 20¢ EACH |
| @ $3.09 | @ $2.09 |

### ❺ SHIPPING AND HANDLING

| Order Total | Add |
|---|---|
| Under $5.00 | $1.50 |
| $5.01-$15.00 | $3.00 |
| $15.01-$35.00 | $4.50 |
| $35.01-$75.00 | $7.00 |
| $75.01-$200.00 | 10% |
| Over $201.00 | 6% |

In addition to the above charges, U.S. territories, HI & AK, add $2.00. Canada & Mexico, add $5.00. Other outside U.S., add $20.00.

Name_____

Affiliation_____

Street_____
P. O. Box numbers not accepted, street address must appear.

City_____ State _____ Zip _____

Phone (_____)_____ Date _____

Method Of Payment Enclosed:    ( ) Check         ( ) Money Order         ( ) Purchase Order

**Prices effective 11/1/95 thru 10/31/96**

## PRIMARY LEVEL... KINDERGARTEN, FIRST, SECOND & THIRD GRADE

| Quantity | ISBN # | Title Description | Unit Price | Total Price |
|---|---|---|---|---|
| | 0-922162-90-5 | "Kumi and Chanti" | | |
| | 0-922162-91-3 | "George Washington Carver" | | |
| | 0-922162-92-1 | "Harriet Tubman" | | |
| | 0-922162-93-X | "Jean Baptist DuSable" | | |
| | 0-922162-94-8 | "Matthew Henson" | | |
| | 0-922162-95-6 | "Bessie Coleman" | | |
| | Total Books | | ❸ Subtotal | |
| | | SEE CHART BELOW ▷ | ❹ IL Residents add 8.75% Sales Tax | |
| | | | ❺ Shipping & Handling | |
| | | | ❻ Total | |

### KEY STEPS IN ORDERING
❶ Establish quantity needs.  ❹ Add tax, if applicable.
❷ Determine book unit price.  ❺ Add shipping &handling.
❸ Determine total cost.  ❻ Total amount.

### BOOK PRICING ● QUANTITY DISCOUNTS
| ❶ Quantity Ordered | ❷ Unit Price |
|---|---|
| 1-49 | $3.49 |
| 50 + | $3.09 |

### ❺ SHIPPING AND HANDLING
| Order Total | Add |
|---|---|
| Under $5 | $1.50 |
| $5.01-$15.00 | $3.00 |
| $15.01- $35.00 | $4.50 |
| $35.01-$75.00 | $7.00 |
| $75.01-$200.00 | 10% |
| Over $201.00 | 6% |

In addition to the above charges, U.S. territories, HI & AK, add $2.00. Canada and Mexico, add $5.00. Other outside U.S., add $20.00.

*Empak Publishing provides attractive counter and floor displays for retailers and organizations interested in the Heritage book series for resale. Please check here ☐ and include this form with your letterhead and we will send you specific information and our special volume discounts.*

• The Empak "Heritage Kids" series provides a basic understanding and appreciation of Black history which translates to cultural awareness, self-esteem, and ethnic pride within young African-American children.

• Assisted by dynamic and impressive 4-color illustrations, readers will be able to relate to the two adorable African kids-- Kumi & Chanti, as they are introduced to the inspirational lives and deeds of significant, historic African-Americans.

# Black History Materials
# Available from Empak Publishing

A Salute To Black History Poster Series
African-American Experience–Period Poster Series
Biographical Poster Series
Heritage Kids Poster Series

Advanced Booklet Series
Instructor's Manuals
Advanced Skills Sheets
Black History Bulletin Board Aids
Instructor's Kits

Intermediate Booklet Series
Teacher's Guides
Intermediate Skill Sheets
Black History Flashcards
Intermediate Reading Certificates
Teacher's Kits

Heritage Kids  Booklet Series
Heritage Kids Resource & Activity Guides
Heritage Kids Reading Certificates
Heritage Kids Kits

Black History Videos
Black History Month Activity & Resource Guide
African-American Times–A Chronological Record
African-American Discovery Board Game
African-American Clip Art
Black History Mugs
Black Heritage Marble Engraving
Black History Month Banners (18" x 60")
Say YES to Black History Education Sweatshirts
Say YES to Black History Education T-Shirts

To receive your copy of the Empak Publishing Company's
colorful new catalog, please send $2 to cover postage and handling to:

Empak Publishing Company
Catalog Dept., Suite 300
212 East Ohio Street
Chicago, IL 60611